WHERE AM I?

In the Forest

Written by Noah Leatherland

Enslow
PUBLISHING

Published in 2025 by Enslow Publishing, LLC
2544 Clinton Street
Buffalo, NY 14224

Written by:
Noah Leatherland

Edited by:
Rebecca Phillips-Bartlett

Designed by:
Amelia Harris

Cataloging-in-Publication Data

Names: Leatherland, Noah, 1999-.
Title: In the forest / Noah Leatherland.
Description: Buffalo, NY : Enslow Publishing, 2025. | Series: Where am I? | Includes glossary.
Identifiers: ISBN 9781978541740 (pbk.) | ISBN 9781978541757 (library bound) | ISBN 9781978541764 (ebook)
Subjects: LCSH: Forest animals--Habitation--Juvenile literature. | Forest animals--Juvenile literature.
Classification: LCC QL112.L38 2025 | DDC 591.73--dc23

Manufactured in the United States of America

CPSIA compliance information: Batch #CW25ENS: For further information contact Enslow Publishing LLC at 1-800-398-2504.

Please visit our website, www.enslowpublishing.com. For a free color catalog of all our high-quality books, call toll free 1-800-398-2504 or fax 1-877-980-4454.

Find us on

PHOTO CREDITS All images are courtesy of Shutterstock.com, unless otherwise specified. With thanks to Getty Images, Thinkstock Photo and iStockphoto.
Recurring – Kashtal, Tartila, Bokeh Blur Background, NMacTavish, Anatolir. Cover – PinkPueblo, Tartila, Erni, DragonTiger8, Rvector, GoodStudio, Kanujan Singarajah, KittyVector, natchapohn, Claudia Pylinskaya, Wirestock Creators. 2–3 – Kawin Jiaranaisakul. 4–5 – Piotr Krzeslak, AustralianCamera. 6–7 – Vaclav Matous, Antonov Maxim, Artfury. 8–9 – Brian Lasenby, Mark Brandon, Magicleaf. 10–11 – Kolesov Sergey, DWI YULIANTO, GoodStudio. 12–13 – Adriana Margarita Larios Arellano, Mufti Adi Utomo, NotionPic, Viktorija Reuta, RealityImages. 14–15 – mlorenz, GoodStudio. 16–17 – natchapohn, PictuLandra, Zane Palma, Isabel Eve, Chris Woodard Photography. 18–19 – johavel, Anna Veselov. 20–21 – TashaBubo, Anthony King Nature, Maquiladora. 22–23 – Sourabh Bharti, Pong Wira, NadiiaKushnyrenko.

CONTENTS

PAGE 4 Where Am I?

PAGE 6 Eurasian Lynx

PAGE 8 Stick Insect

PAGE 10 Long-Nosed Horned Frog

PAGE 12 Vine Snake

PAGE 14 Great Horned Owl

PAGE 16 Blue Morpho Butterfly

PAGE 18 Leaf-Tailed Gecko

PAGE 20 Green Woodpecker

PAGE 22 Hiding in the Habitat

PAGE 24 Glossary and Index

WHERE AM I?

Welcome to the forest! Forest habitats are full of life. Forests are areas with lots of trees and other kinds of plants growing down below.

A habitat is where an animal lives and has everything they need to survive.

Forests are usually home to lots of different animals. They have plenty of food that is perfect for many animals. Forests also give animals places to hide when they do not want to be seen.

EURASIAN LYNX

I am a Eurasian lynx. I can be found in forests across Europe and Asia. Forest environments change with the seasons. I change the color of my fur to keep myself camouflaged as the seasons change.

During the summer months, I have brown fur. In the winter, my fur turns gray to match the snowy environment. This helps me hide from my prey.

STICK INSECT

I am a stick insect. I am a master of camouflage. My body looks just like a stick. I climb on branches and move very slowly to blend into my surroundings. This helps me hide from predators.

I gently sway side to side when I move around. This makes it look like I am just a stick blowing in the wind. Sometimes, my eggs are camouflaged by looking like seeds.

LONG-NOSED HORNED FROG

I am a long-nosed horned frog. Since forests have so many trees, there are usually a lot of fallen leaves on the ground. I use these fallen leaves to hide.

I have brown patterns on my back and have pointy horns on my head. It makes me look like an old, dead leaf. This helps me hide from other animals.

VINE SNAKE

I am a vine snake. Instead of slithering along the ground, I climb up trees. The color of my scales helps me camouflage myself in the branches. I can blend in with the branches or the leaves.

Sometimes, I lure in prey with my tongue. I move my tongue very slowly to make it look like a worm. This tricks my prey into getting close enough for me to strike.

GREAT HORNED OWL

I am a great horned owl. I am an excellent hunter. I have long claws called talons that help me snatch up prey. My soft feathers help me fly very quietly so that my prey does not hear me coming.

The color of my feathers helps me to camouflage myself. My feathers are usually brown and white. This makes it easy for me to blend in with the trees I nest in.

BLUE MORPHO BUTTERFLY

I am a blue morpho butterfly. My wings are blue on one side and brown on the other. When I fly, the colors confuse other animals. It looks like I am disappearing and appearing again!

The brown side of my wings have circle patterns. These patterns are called eyespots. They look like the eyes of predators. This scares other animals and keeps them away from me.

How many eyespots does my wing have?

LEAF-TAILED GECKO

I am a leaf-tailed gecko. Can you guess where I got my name from? My tail looks just like a leaf! This lets me blend in with the leaves of the forest I live in.

It is not just my tail that helps me camouflage myself. I can flatten my body against tree trunks. When I do this, I am very hard to spot!

GREEN WOODPECKER

I am a green woodpecker. Many birds make their nests in tree branches. I use my strong beak to make holes inside tree trunks to nest in. It is a perfect hiding spot.

I spend a lot of time on the ground looking for food. My green feathers help me camouflage myself with the green grass. This helps me hide from predators while I look for food.

HIDING IN THE HABITAT

A lot of the time, animals do not want to be seen. Hiding helps animals survive. Some animals hide from predators, some hide from their prey, and some hide from both.

A TIGER HIDING IN THE GRASS

Can you think of any other animals that hide or camouflage themselves? Have you ever seen them? You might have seen one, but they were so well camouflaged that you did not notice!

GLOSSARY

CAMOUFLAGED blended in with the surroundings

ENVIRONMENTS the surroundings in which an animal or plant lives or spends time

LURE to encourage something to come closer

PREDATORS animals that hunt other animals for food

PREY animals that are hunted by other animals for food

INDEX

BEAKS 20

EGGS 9

FEATHERS 14–15, 21

FUR 6–7

GRASS 21–22

LEAVES 10–12, 18

TALONS 14

TREES 4, 10, 12, 15, 19–20

WINGS 16–17